NICOLA PATTERNS

presents

SOCKS FOR DOLLS

Fully Fashioned Knitting Patterns
based on original antique socks
To fit 7" to 26" Dolls

Joan Nerini

TAFFETA PUBLICATIONS

DEDICATION

To Nicola, my granddaughter.

Sock Design and Text: Joan Nerini © Copyright 1994.
Book and Photo Design: Ferini Designs, Lowestoft, Suffolk.
Photography: Paul Hobbs

First edition printed in Great Britain. 1994
by Asgard Printing, Lowestoft, Suffolk.
for Taffeta Publications.
Brighton, East Sussex, England.

ISBN 0 9512835 2 9

All rights reserved. No part of this publication may be reproduced, stored in a retrieval system, or transmitted, in any form or by any means, electronic, mechanical, photocopying, recording or otherwise, without the prior permission of the copyright owner.

Front Cover Photograph - Doll by Gina Saunders.
Back Cover Photograph - Dolls by Gillie Charlson.
All three dolls dressed by Joan Nerini
Knitting needles and thread available by mail order - see Page 39.

CONTENTS

Introduction			4
General Hints			6
1.	Socks with vertical fancy design.	to fit 26" doll.	11
2.	Socks in plain stocking stitch with decorative clocks.	to fit 22/24" doll.	14
3.	Socks in stocking stitch background with eyelet holes.	to fit 20/21" doll.	17
4.	Socks with diamond lace design.	to fit 18/19" doll.	20
5.	Socks in plain stocking stitch with shaped leg	to fit 16" doll.	23
6.	Socks with vertical plain and fancy rib.	to fit 15" doll.	26
7.	Socks with diagonal openwork broken rib.	to fit 13/14" doll.	29
8.	Socks with openwork mesh.	to fit 11" doll.	32
9.	Socks with diagonal fancy rib.	to fit 9/10" doll.	34
10.	Socks with narrow contrast stripes.	to fit 7" doll.	36
Abbreviations and Conversion into Metric			38

INTRODUCTION

Following on from the knitting patterns for large and small dolls which were produced within the range of NICOLA Patterns, I have now designed some new knitting patterns for a variety of socks to fit dolls from 7" to 26" (head-to-toe). The designs for the larger socks are more elaborate than the previous patterns and are based on the shapes and stitches found on original antique dolls of the 19th Century.

Most of the commercial socks worn by these dolls were machine made with a very fine tension in silk or cotton thread. A great many elaborate stitch designs were created as well as simple openwork weaves and plain stocking stitch fabric. The colours were mainly cream, pale blue or pink, but there were variations of coloured stripes, bordered tops and plain black, or brown.

I have been lucky enough to obtain and also borrow several original dolls' socks of the 19th Century and have endeavoured to reproduce them for you to knit. In some of the designs the top of the sock has a knitted rib, whereas others have the picot-edged hem which is so often seen on the socks worn by the more expensive French dolls. I found several different ways of shaping for the heel and foot on the original socks, and I have included these in some of the designs. They may be new to some of you as they were to me.

The knitting patterns have been designed with various thickness of thread and size of needle to give you a choice of texture and delicacy of design. I have also included leg and foot measurements of the average doll each sock should fit. All the socks in this book are knitted on two needles and sewn together with a back and undersole seam.

Where the foot shaping follows the antique style of sock you will find extra seams along the instep and undersole but I have written the making-up instructions in great detail so that you will understand how to join up the foot section.

The fully fashioned shaping of the heel and toe in these patterns will enable a shoe to fit snugly over the sock. No more bulky wrinkled socks which need a larger shoe to fit !!

Because these socks are handknitted there is greater elasticity than a modern purchased fabric sock would have. Therefore there will be a certain amount of flexibility of fit - possibly up to half-an-inch depending on the tension of your knitting. However, remember that should the width of knitting be fully stretched around the doll's leg, the overall length of the sock could become shorter than the original knitted measurement.

The knitting tension used to produce each sock is given at the beginning of each instruction so that should you wish to knit any design in a finer or thicker needle and thread you will be able to calculate the addition or subtraction of stitches to achieve the same size of sock. Further help on how to achieve this is given in the following chapter on General Hints.

~ ~ ~ ~ ~ ~ ~ ~ ~ ~ ~ ~ ~ ~ ~ ~ ~

GENERAL HINTS

Tension
(The number of stitches and rows achieved in a 1" square of knitted fabric).

The combination of a particular size of needle and thickness of thread will produce a knitted fabric with certain measurements over a number of stitches and a number of rows. This represents the tension and will help to calculate the size of the finished garment. Once you know the finished measurements required, you can then to calculate the number of stitches and the number of rows which will produce the correct garment.

A tension swatch using other needles and/or thread than the suggested materials in any pattern will give you a different number of stitches and rows over one inch to enable you to either produce a smaller or larger sock or to decrease or increase the number of stitches and rows to suit your new measurement.

The tension of the knitting used to produce each sock is given at the beginning of each instruction.

Using the suggested thread and knitting pins the finished sock should fit the leg and foot measurements of the particular doll they are designed for. If you are unfamiliar with knitting with fine needles and thread, I would suggest that you knit a swatch to test your tension before beginning any particular sock.

Prepare a swatch for tension :

Cast on 20 sts. Work 4 rows garter stitch and then work 24 rows in stocking stitch. Work a further 4 rows garter stitch and cast off.
The garter stitch at beginning and end will stop the small piece of knitted fabric from curling and make it easier to measure the tension produced.

Using Fine Knitting Pins

When using fine knitting pins of sizes 18 or 20 or even 22, you may have to adopt a slightly different position of the needles in your hands to prevent your fingers being pricked by the fine points. Hold the needles so that the points cross on top of the first finger, keeping the knitting close to the pointed ends so that the stitches can be drawn off the needle with ease. Also hold the knitting already made with your left hand close up to the needle (or vice versa if you are lefthanded). This will help steady your work while knitting as the fine fabric produced is very light.

The thread suggested with a particular size of needle should be used whenever possible, as any thicker thread will make the stitches tighter on the needle and difficult to draw off. Too thick a thread is also often the cause of the needles becoming bent when too much pressure is used to move the stitches. Likewise a thicker needle with very fine thread will produce a very loose tension and a lacy design can look untidy. As long as the thread is in proportion to the thickness of the needle, then you will find you can knit as normally as you would for a lifesize garment when you are more likely to be working with a thick needle and double knitting wool. It will however take a little practice to get accustomed to the lightness of the work.

Take the first few rows of your work slowly because there is very little knitted fabric to hold in your hand to steady the rythmn of your knitting and produce an even tension. *Believe me, the first four rows are the worst!!*

Any dropped stitches at this early stage are almost impossible to pick up when so few rows are worked. If this is your first experience with fine knitting then please do not give up at this stage as the end result of delicate fancy or openwork socks will reward your patience and practice.

Using Fine Needles and Thread for the first time.

It is advisable to work on white or light coloured thread rather than any that is dark or even black. Try out the stitches of a pattern on a small piece of knitting and practice the sequence of rows before starting on the actual sock. Your practice and patient effort will be rewarded when you finish knitting your authentic reproduction socks and fit them on your doll.

Stopping your work in the middle of a row.
If you get interrupted when knitting on fine steel needles, try to complete the row as the middle stitches can stretch when two needles are folded with the row incomplete. Such stretched stitches are very noticable and could spoil your even tension. If you have to stop and put your work down in the middle of a row, then please return to finish that row as soon as possible. Also if you get interrupted when working on a fancy stitch, try to mark your pattern, or write down the row you have just worked so that you can resume the design with ease on returning to your knitting.

Dropped Stitches
Unfortunately, dropping a stitch is a hazard when using fine thread and steel pin-like needles. Holding the worked knitted fabric close to the needle with your left hand as you knit will help to hold a dropped stitch from falling further down a stocking stitch fabric.

Use another needle, or crochet hook to halt the dropped stitch and bring it back onto the working needle. If, however, the dropped stitch is in an openwork design and has fallen to a decreased stitch and 'disappeared', then you should go back and unpick the last two rows carefully until you find the 'lost' stitch and then continue as before.

Suggesting that you unpick your work may seem rather heartless but it is well worth the effort, especially when you are at the end of the lace knitting section. Take care when undoing decreased stitches as one may drop. If this happens, pinch the area with your thumb and forefinger to catch the 'elusive' stitch before further damage is done. You may find that the undone stitches on the final row are 'back to front' when restarting normal knitting. Bring each stitch to the right slant before working as a twisted stitch will distort the look of a fancy design.

Diagonal Rib
Some of the designs have a pattern stitch which creates an openwork diagonal rib and causes your knitting edges to slant. This is quite normal and characteristic of this type of design. When joining the back seam, it will be at an angle across the sock and not straight at centre back. Take care to make a neat join which will not be noticeable in the slant of the rib.

Decreasing
When using most of these patterns you will notice that I have used the "slip one, knit one, pass slipped stitch over" method for decreasing and shaping wherever possible. This is because it is easier to decrease in this manner rather than knitting two stitches together when using fine needles and thread. The exception is when a fancy or openwork design requires the threads to slope in each direction then both methods of decreasing are necessary in any one row.

Increasing
In a fancy or openwork design, it is necessary to make a stitch to create the eyelet holes. Every 'made' stitch is counteracted by a decrease to keep the number of stitches on the needle constant. Such decreases will occur in the same row but occasionally you can find them in the following row.

There are 4 ways to make a stitch depending on the stitch which preceeds and follows it. In these patterns only the YF (yarn forward) is used but the following notes will clarify each process for 'making' a stitch when you come across these initials in some other lacy design which you may choose.

yf = yarn forward.
This instruction is given to make a stitch between two Knit stitches. When the first Knit stitch is worked the yarn is at the back of your work and would normally remain there for the following Knit stitch. It is therefore necessary to bring the yarn forward to the front and as you knit the next stitch the yarn creates an unworked stitch over the righthand needle.

yon = yarn over needle.
This instruction is given to make a stitch

between a Purl stitch and a Knit stitch. When the first Purl stitch is worked the yarn is at the front of your work and would be taken to the back under the needle for the next Knit stitch. It is therefore necessary to keep the yarn at the front and bring it over the needle to the back to work the next knit stitch thereby creating an unworked stitch over the righthand needle.

yfrn = yarn forward and round needle.
This instruction is given to make a stitch between a Knit and a Purl stitch. When the first Knit stitch is worked the yarn is at the back of your work and would be taken to the front under the needle. It is therefore necessary to bring the yarn forward under the needle and then round the needle to the front again to work the next Purl stitch. Bringing the yarn around the needle creates an unworked stitch over the righthand needle.

yrn = yarn round needle.
This instruction is given to make a stitch between two Purl stitches. The yarn is forward for the first Purl stitch and would normally remain at the front for the second Purl stitch. It is therefore necessary to take the yarn round the needle and bring it to the front to create an unworked stitch over the righthand needle. On any return row, all 'made' stitches from the row before must be worked as an actual stitch to create the eyelet hole in the design.

Changing the pattern design
There are many stitch designs which would be suitable for dolls' socks. A good reference book on Knitting Stitches will provide you with a whole range of new ideas. Your library or bookshop may well have such a book on their shelves. Choose a design that has a smaller number of rows to repeat the whole pattern in depth as the number of rows for a normal sock may not be more than 50 (top to ankle). Also a smaller number of stitches to one repeat pattern is more in proportion to the width of a doll's leg. If the number of stitches in any one of the patterns does not divide evenly with a new pattern repeat, then it is permissible to add up to 4 stitches across the width to fit in the repeat and still not affect the overall fit of the sock. If in doubt work a tension swatch to check your measurement.

SOCK No.1

Socks with vertical fancy design. Picot edged top and fully fashioned heel.

To fit a 26" Doll
or Doll with approx. leg and foot measurements:
Around Calf: 6¾"
Around Ankle: 5"
Instep (centre leg to toe): 2"
Ankle to Floor: 1"
Knee Joint to Floor (side): 6"
Sole (toe to heel): 3¼"

No. 1.
Socks with vertical fancy design.
Picot edged top and fully fashioned square shaped heel.
(See Photograph and Measurements on previous page)

Materials:
1 (20 gram) ball Cotton Thread No. 40.
1 pair Knitting Pins. Size 18.

Tension: 16 sts & 20 rows to 1" over st.st.

Instructions:
Cast on 75 sts.
Work top for a picot-edged hem thus:
Work 12 rows in st st.
Next row: K1, * yf, k2tog, repeat from * to last st, k1.
Next row: K1, purl to last st, k1.
Work 12 rows in k1, p1, rib.
Change to pattern:
Row 1. K2, * wf, k2, sl1, k2tog, psso, k2, wf, k1, repeat from * to last st. k1.
Row 2 K1, purl to last st., k1.
Repeat these 2 rows of pattern 56 times, and dec. one stitch at end of last pattern row.
Shape fully fashioned square heel:
Change to st st.
K22 turn, sl1 purlwise, p20, k1.
Work a further 24 rows in this manner on these 22 sts.
Next 2 rows: K10, k2tog, turn, P10, k1.
Next 2 rows: K10 k2tog, turn, P10 k1.
Continue decreasing in this manner until 11 sts remain on needle.
Next row: K11, pick up and knit 14 sts through slipped sts, pattern 30 sts, k22.
Reverse shaping for other side of heel:
Next row: K1, p21, turn, sl1, k21.
Work a further 24 rows in this manner on these 22 sts.
Next 2 rows: K1, p9, p2tog, turn - knit to end.
Next 2 rows: K1, p9 p2tog, turn - knit to end.
Continue decreasing in this manner until 11 sts remain on needle.
Next row: K1, p10, pick up and purl 14 sts through slipped sts, p54, k1.
Keeping 25 sts at either side in st st, and centre 30 sts in pattern, work 20 more rows straight.

Next row: K1, sl1, k1, psso, k20, sl1, k1, psso, pattern 30, k2tog, k20, k2tog, k1.
Work 3 rows straight.
Next row: K1, sl1, k1, psso, k18, sl1, k1, psso, pattern 30, k2tog, k18, k2tog, k1.
Work 3 rows straight.
Next row: K1, sl1, k1, psso, k16, sl1, k1, psso, pattern 30, k2tog, k16, k2tog, k1.

Shape for toe:
Row 1: K3, * sl1, k1, psso, k6, repeat from * to last st, k1.
Row 2 and every alternate row: K1, purl to last st. k1.
Row 3: K3, * sl1, k1, psso, k5, repeat from * to last st, k1.
Row 5: K3, * sl1, k1, psso, k4, repeat from * to last st, k1.
Row 7: K3, * sl1, k1, psso, k3, repeat from * to last st, k1.
Row 9: K3, sl1, k1, psso, k2, repeat from * to last st, k1.
Row 11: K3, * sl1, k1, psso, k1, repeat from * to end.
Row 13: K1, * sl1, k1, psso, repeat from * to end.
Row 15: K1, *sl1, k1, psso, repeat from * to last st, k1.
Break thread. Draw thread through remaining sts.

To make up:

With right sides together, join sole, heel and back seam, taking care to have heel shaping and top hemline even on both sides.

To form picot-edged top hem: Fold top to wrong side along first line of holes. To fasten hem, loosely slipstitch cast-on edge just above first row of pattern. Turn sock to right side and press.

SOCK No.2

Plain socks in stocking stitch with decorative clocks at sides. Fully fashioned diagonal shaped heel.

To fit a 22"/24" Doll
or Doll with approx. leg and foot measurements:
Around Calf: 6½"
Around Ankle: 5"
Instep (centre leg to toe): 2"
Ankle to Floor: 1"
Knee Joint to Floor (side): 5½"
Sole (toe to heel): 3"

No 2.
Socks in plain stocking stitch with decorative clocks at sides. Fully fashioned diagonal shaped heel.
(See Photograph and Measurements on page opposite)

Materials:
1 (20 gram.) ball Cotton Thread No. 40
1 pair Knitting Pins. Size 16.

Tension: 12 sts and 16 rows to 1".

Instructions:
Cast on 58 sts. (**) Work 18 rows in k1, p1 rib.
(**)Alternatively, work top with a picot-edged hem. - See Basic Instruction on Page 25.
Work 22 rows in st st straight.

The following instructions create the decorative clocks at either side of sock leg.
Row 1. K15, sl1, k1, psso, yf, k24, yf, k2tog, k.15.
Row 2 and every alternate row. K1, purl to last st. k1.
Row 3. K14, sl1, k1, psso, yf, k1, yf, k2tog, k20, sl1, k1, psso, yf, k1, yf, k2tog, k14.
Row 5. K13, sl1, k1, psso, yf, k3, yf, k2tog, k.18, sl1, k1, psso, yf, k3, yf, k2tog, k13.
Rows 7 to 30. Repeat Rows 1 & 2 - 12 times.
Now continue in plain stocking stitch.

Shape heel:
K18 turn, sl1 purlwise, purl to last st, k1.
K17 turn, sl1 purlwise, purl to last st. k1.
K16 turn, sl1 purlwise, purl to last st. k1.
Continue to shape heel in this manner until 6 sts are on needle.

Now reverse shaping:
K6, pick up loop from row below and k2tog with the next stitch on lefthand needle, turn, sl1 purlwise, purl to last st. k1.
Next row: K7, pick up loop from row below and k2tog, with next stitch on lefthand needle, turn, sl1 purlwise, purl to last st, k1.
Repeat in this manner until all 18 sts are on needle and continue to knit across remaining 38 sts.

Shape other side of heel:
P18 turn, sl1, knit to end.
P17 turn, sl1, knit to end.
P16 turn, sl1, knit to end. Continue to shape heel in this manner until 6 sts. are on needle.

Now reverse shaping:
P6, pick up loop from row below and p2tog with next stitch on lefthand needle, turn, sl1, knit to end.
Next row: P7, pick up loop from row below and p2tog, with next stitch on lefthand needle, turn, sl1, knit to end.
Repeat in this manner until all 18 sts. are back on needle.
Continuing in st st., work a further 13 rows straight across all sts.
Next row: K16, sl1, k1, psso, k22, k2tog, k16. Work 3 rows straight.
Next row: K15, sl1, k1, psso, k22, k2tog, k15. Work 3 rows straight.
Next row: K14, sl1, k1, psso, k22, k2tog, k14.
Next row: K1, purl to last st. k1.

Shape for toe:
Row 1:* K2,sl1,k1,psso,k6, repeat from * to end.
Row 2 and every alternate row: K1, purl to last st, k1.
Row 3: * K2, sl1, k1, psso, k5, repeat from * to end.
Row 5: * K2, sl1, k1, psso, k4, repeat from * to end.
Row 7: * K2, sl1, k1, psso, k3, repeat from * to end.
Row 9: * K2, sl1, k1, psso, k2, repeat from * to end.
Row 11: *K1, sl1, k1, psso, k1,repeat from * to end.
Row 13: Repeat Row 11.
Break thread and draw through remaining sts.

To make up:
With right sides together, join sole, heel and back seam, taking care to have heel shaping and decorative clocks even on both sides. Turn sock to right side and press seams.
If an alternative picot-edged top has been worked, complete hem thus: Fold top to wrong side along first line of holes. To fasten hem, loosely slipstitch cast-on edge just above next line of holes. Turn sock to right side and press.

SOCK No.3

Socks in stocking stitch with alternate rows of eyelet holes. Fully fashioned diagonal shaped heel.

To fit a 20"/21" Doll
or Doll with approx. leg and foot measurements:

Around Calf:	6"
Around Ankle:	4$\frac{3}{4}$"
Instep (centre leg to toe):	1$\frac{3}{4}$"
Ankle to Floor:	$\frac{3}{4}$"
Knee Joint to Floor (side):	5"
Sole (toe to heel):	2$\frac{3}{4}$"

No. 3.
Socks in stocking stitch with alternate rows of eyelet holes. Fully fashioned diagonal shaped heel.
(See Photograph and Measurements on previous page)

Materials:
1 (20 gram) ball Cotton Thread No. 40.
1 pair Knitting Pins. Size 18.

Tension: 16 sts and 20 rows to 1" over st st.

Instructions:
Cast on 62 sts.(**) Work 20 rows in k1, p1 rib
(**) *Alternatively, work top with a picot-edged hem. - See Basic Instruction on Page 25.*
Change to pattern:
Row 1: * K4, yf, sl1, k1, psso, repeat from * to last 2 sts, k2.
Row 2: K1, purl to last st, k1.
Row 3: K1, * yf, sl1, k1, psso, k4, repeat from * to last st, k1.
Row 4: As Row 2.
Repeat these 4 rows - 12 times.

Shape heel (worked in st.st.):
K18 turn, sl1 purlwise, purl to last st, k1.
K17 turn, sl1 purlwise, purl to last st, k1.
K16 turn, sl1 purlwise, purl to last st, k1.
Continue to shape heel in this manner until 6 sts. are on needle.
Now reverse shaping:
K6, pick up the loop from row below and k2tog with the next stitch on lefthand needle, turn, sl1, purlwise, purl to last st, k1.
K7, pick up loop from row below and k2tog, with next stitch on lefthand needle, turn, sl1, purlwise, purl to last st, k1.
Continue in this manner until all 18 sts are on needle.
Next row: K18, pattern 26, k18.
Shape other side of heel:
P18 turn, sl1, knit to end.
P17 turn, sl1, knit to end.
P16 turn, sl1, knit to end. Continue to shape heel in this manner until 6 sts. are on needle.
Now reverse shaping:
P6, pick up loop from row below and p2tog, with next stitch on lefthand needle, turn, sl1, knit to end.

P7, pick up loop from row below and p2tog, with next stitch on lefthand needle, turn, sl1, knit to end.
Continue in this manner until all 18 sts are on needle.
Next row: K1, purl to last st, k1.
Work a further 12 rows straight, keeping centre 26 sts in pattern and 18 sts at either end in st st.
Next row: K16, sl1, k1, psso, pattern 26, k2tog, k16.
Work 3 rows straight, keeping centre pattern rows correct.
Next row: K15, sl1, k1, psso, pattern 26, k2tog, k15.
Work 3 rows straight, keeping centre pattern rows correct.
Next row: K14, sl1, k1, psso, pattern 26, k2tog, k14.
Next row: K1, purl to last st. k1.

Shape for toe:
Row 1: * K2, sl1, k1, psso, k6, repeat from * to last 4 sts, k4.
Row 2 and every alternate row: K1, purl to last st, k1.
Row 3: * K2, sl1, k1, psso, k5, repeat from * to last 3 sts, k3.
Row 5: * K2, sl1, k1, psso, k4, repeat from * to last 2 sts, k2.
Row 7: * K2, sl1, k1, psso, k3, repeat from * to last st, k1.
Row 9: * K2, sl1, k1, psso, k2, repeat from * to end.
Row 11: K2, * sl1, k1, psso, k1, repeat from * last st, k1.
Row 13: K1, * sl1, k1, psso, repeat from * to end. Break thread. Draw thread through remaining sts.

To make up:

With right sides together, join sole, heel and back seam, taking care to keep heel shaping and top ribbing (or hemline) even on both sides. Turn sock to right side and press.
If an alternative picot-edged top has been worked, complete hem thus: Fold top to wrong side along first line of holes. To fasten hem, loosely slipstitch cast-on edge just above next line of holes. Turn sock to right side and press.

SOCK No. 4

Socks with diamond lace design. Picot edged top and fully fashioned diagonal shaped heel.

To fit a 18"/19" Doll
or Doll with approx. leg and foot measurements:
Around Calf: 5"
Around Ankle: 4"
Instep (centre leg to toe): 1½"
Ankle to Floor: ¾"
Knee Joint to Floor (side): 4½"
Sole (toe to heel): 2⅜"

No. 4.

Socks with diamond lace design. Picot edged top and fully fashioned diagonal shaped heel.
(See Photograph and Measurements on page opposite)

Materials:
1 (20 gram) ball Cotton Thread No.40.
1 pair Knitting Pins. Size 18.

Tension: 16 sts and 20 rows to 1" over st st.

Instructions:
Cast on 48 sts.
Work top for a picot-edged hem thus:
Row 1: Knit. **Row 2:** K1, purl to last st, k1.
Rows 3-10: Repeat Rows 1 & 2 four times.
Row 11: * K1, yf, sl1, k1, psso., repeat from * to last st, k1.
Row 12: K1, purl to last st, k1.
Rows 13-22: Repeat Rows 1 to 10 once.
Change to pattern:
Row 1: K2, * k4, yf, sl1, k1, psso, k2tog, yf, repeat from * to last 6 sts, k6
Row 2: K1, purl to last st, k1.
Rows 3 & 4: Repeat Rows 1 & 2.
Row 5: K2, * yf, sl1, k1, psso, k2tog, yf, k4, repeat from * to last 6 sts, yf, sl1, k1, psso, k2tog, yf, k2.
Row 6: K1, purl to last st, k1.
Rows 7 & 8: Repeat Rows 5 & 6.
Repeat pattern Rows 1-8 four times.

Shape for heel:
K12, turn, sl1 purlwise, p10, kl.
K11, turn, sl1 purlwise, p9. k1.
K10, turn, sl1 purlwise, p8. k1.
K9, turn, sl1 purlwise, p7, k1.
K8, turn, sl1 purlwise, p6, k1.
K7, turn, sl1 purlwise, p5, k1.

Now reverse shaping:
K6, pick up loop from work below and k2tog with the next stitch on lefthand needle, turn, sl1 purlwise, p5, k1.
K7, pick up loop from work below and k2tog with next stitch on lefthand needle, turn, sl1 purlwise, p6, k1.
Continue in this manner until all 12 sts. are back on needle.
Next row: K12, pattern 24, k12.

Shape other side of heel :
K1, p11, turn, sl1, k11.
K1, p10, turn, sl1, k.10.
K1, p9, turn, sl1, k9.
Continue in this manner until 6 sts. are on needle.

Now reverse shaping to match other heel until 12 sts. are back on needle.
Next row: K1., purl to last st, k1.
Continue straight for foot and work 24 rows on these 48 sts, keeping the centre 24 sts. in pattern and the 12 sts. on either side in st st. (Three repeat pattern Rows 1-8).

Shape for toe:
Change to st.st.
Row 1:. * K5, sl1, k1, psso, repeat from * to last 6 sts, k4, sl1, k1, psso.
Rows 2, 4, 6, & 8. K1, purl to last st, k1.
Row 3: * K4, sl1, k1, psso., repeat from * to last 5 sts., k3, sl1, k1, psso.
Row 5: * K3, sl1, k1, psso., repeat from * to last 4 sts., k2, sl1, k1, psso.
Row 7: * K2, sl1, k1, psso., repeat from * to last 3 sts., k1, sl1, k1, psso.

Row 9: * Kl, sl1, k1, psso., to end.
Break thread.
Draw thread through remaining sts.

To make up:

With right sides together, join sole, heel and back seam, taking care to have heel shaping and top hemline even on both sides. Turn sock to right side and press.

To form picot-edged hem at top, fold top to wrong side along first line of holes. Slipstitch cast-on edge loosely just above first row of pattern. Turn sock to right side and press.

SOCK No.5

Socks in plain stocking stitch. Shaped leg to slim ankle. Ribbed top and fully fashioned square shaped heel.

To fit a 16" Doll
or Doll with approx. leg and foot measurements:

Around Calf:	4 3/4"
Around Ankle:	3 3/4"
Instep (centre leg to toe):	1 1/4"
Ankle to Floor:	5/8"
Knee Joint to Floor (side):	4 1/4"
Sole (toe to heel):	2 1/4"

No.5
Socks in plain stocking stitch.
Shaped leg to slim ankle. Ribbed top and fully fashioned square shaped heel.
(See Photograph and Measurements on previous page)

Materials:
1 (20 gram) ball Cotton Thread No.40.
1 pair Knitting Pins. Size 18.

Tension: 16 sts and 20 rows to 1" over st st.

Instructions:
Cast on 60 sts.
Work k1, p1 rib for 16 rows.
Change to st st, but work a knit st at beg and end of every purl row.
Work 24 rows straight.
Next row: K1, s1, k1, psso, k54, k2tog, k1.
Continue to decrease one st at either end of every following 4th row until 44 sts remain.
Next row: K1, purl to last st, k1.
Shape for fully fashioned square heel:
K14 turn. Sl1 purlwise, p12, k1.
Repeat these rows until 12 rows have been worked on these 14 sts.
Next 2 rows: K5, k2tog, turn. Purl to last st, k1.
Next 2 rows: K5, k2tog, turn. Purl to last st, k1.
Continue to decrease in this manner until 6 sts are on needle.
Next row: K6, pick up 8 sts through slipped stitches on side of heel, k to end.
Shape other heel:
K1, purl 13 turn. Sl1, k13.
Work 12 more rows in this manner on these 14 sts.
Next 2 rows: K1, p4, p2tog, turn, knit to end.
Next 2 rows: K1, p4, p2tog, turn, knit to end.
Continue to decrease in this manner until 6 sts are on needle.
Next row: K1, p5, pick up and purl 8 sts through slipped stitches on side of heel, purl to last st, k1.
Work 20 rows straight.
Shape for toe:
lst row: * K6, sl1, k1, psso, repeat from * to last 4 sts, k4.
2nd row and every alternate row: K1, purl to last st, k1.

3rd row: * K5, sl1, k1, psso, repeat from * to last 4 sts,. k4.
5th row: * K4, sl1, k1, psso, repeat from * to last 4 sts, k4.
7th row: * K3, sl1, k1, psso, repeat from * to last 4 sts, k4.
9th row: * K2, sl1. k1, psso, repeat from * to end.
11th row: * K1, sl1, k1, psso., repeat to end.
13th row: * Sl1, k1, psso, repeat to end.
Break thread. Draw thread through remaining sts.

To make up:

With right sides together, pin sock together along sole and heel seam and continue up back seam matching shaping of heel and leg. Starting at the toe, stitch total seam.
Turn sock to right side and press.

Basic Instructions to make a Picot-edged Hem at the top of a Sock.

Cast on an even number of stitches.
If the subsequent pattern requires an uneven number of stitches then dec 1 st at the end of the last purl row.
Work 8/10/12 rows in st st, depending on the size of the doll and depth of hem required.
Next row: K1,* yr, sl1, k1, psso, repeat from * to last st, k1.
Next row: K1, purl to last st, k1.
Work 8/10/12 rows (the same number as chosen above) in either st st, or k1, p1 rib. Alternatively, these last set of rows can be worked in a diagonal rib as follows:
Ist row: K1,* yf, sl1, k1, psso, k1, repeat from * to end. **2nd row:** K1, purl to last st, k1.
Repeat these two rows as required.
Next row: K1, * yf, sl1, k1, psso, repeat from * to last st, k1.
Next row: K1, purl to last st, k1.

Continue to knit the length of the sock leg in either st st, or any other fancy or lacy stitch pattern.

SOCK No.6

Socks with vertical plain and fancy rib. Picot-edged top and fully fashioned square shaped heel.

To fit a 15" Doll
or Doll with approx. leg and foot measurements:

Around Calf:	4"
Around Ankle:	3"
Instep (centre leg to toe):	1"
Ankle to Floor:	3/4"
Knee Joint to Floor (side):	3½"
Sole (toe to heel):	1½"

No.6
Socks with vertical plain and fancy rib.
(See photograph and Measurements on opposite page)

Materials:
1 ball DMC No. 80 Thread.
1 pair Knitting Pins. Size 20.

Tension: 18 sts and 22 rows to 1" over st st.

Instructions:
Cast on 64 sts.
Work a picot-edged top thus:
Work 12 rows in st st.
Row 13: K1, * yf, sl1, k1, psso, repeat from * to last st, k1.
Row 14: K1, purl to last st, k1.
Rows 15 - 26: Work 12 rows in k1, p1 rib.
Rows 27 & 28: Repeat Rows 13 & 14.
Change to pattern:
lst row: K3, * yf, sl1, k1, psso, k5 repeat from * to last 5 sts, yf, sl1, k1, psso, k3.
2nd row: K1, purl to last st., k1.
3rd row: K3, * sl1, k1, psso, yf, k5, repeat from * to last 5 sts, sl1, k1, psso, yf, k3.
4th row: As 2nd row.
Repeat these 4 rows of pattern 4 times.
Continue with the pattern but at the same time, decrease one st at the beginning and end of the next and every alternate row until 44 sts remain.
Next row: As 4th row.

Shape for square fully fashioned heel:
Next row: K14 turn.
Next row: Sl1, p12, k1.
Repeat these last 2 rows until 16 rows have been worked on these 14 sts.
Next row: K5, k2tog., turn.
Next row: Purl to last st. k.1.
Next row: K5, k.2 tog., turn.
Next row: Purl to last st. k.1.
Continue to decrease in this manner until 6 sts are on needle.
Next row: Purl to last st. k.1.
Next row: K6, pick up 8 sts. through slipped stitches on side of heel, pattern 16 sts. k14.

Shape other heel:
Next row: K1, p13 turn.
Next row: Sl1, k13.

Repeat these last 2 rows until 16 rows have been worked on these 14 sts.
Next row: K1, p4, p2tog, turn.
Next row: Knit.
Next row: K1, p4, p2tog, turn.
Next row: Knit.
Continue to decrease in this manner until 6 sts are on needle.
Next row: K1, p5, pick up and purl 8 sts. through slipped stitches on side of heel, purl to last st, k1.
Keeping 14 sts on either side of work in st st and centre 16 sts in pattern, work 20 more rows.

Shape for toe:
lst row: * K6, sl1, k1, psso, repeat from * to last 4 sts, k4.
2nd row and every alternate row: K1, purl to last st, k1.
3rd row: * K5, sl1, k1, psso, repeat from * to last 4 sts, k4.
5th row: * K4, sl1, k1, psso, repeat from * to last 4 sts, k4.
7th row: * K3, sl1, k1, psso, repeat from * to last 4 sts, k4.
9th row: * K2, sl1, k1, psso, repeat from * to end.
11th row: * K1, sl1, k1, psso, repeat to end.
13th row: * Sl1, k1, psso, repeat to end.
Break thread. Draw thread through remaining sts.

To make up:

With right sides together, pin sock together along sole and heel seam and continue up back seam matching shaping and pattern carefully. Starting at the toe, stitch total seam.

To form picot-edged hem at top, fold top to wrong side along first line of holes. Slipstitch cast-on edge loosely just above second row of holes.
Turn sock to right side and press.

SOCK No.7

Socks with diagonal openwork broken rib. Picot-edged top and shaped foot (antique style).

To fit a 13"/14" Doll
or Doll with approx. leg and foot measurements:

Around Calf:	3¾"
Around Ankle:	2¾"
Instep (centre leg to toe):	¾"
Ankle to Floor:	½"
Knee Joint to Floor (side):	3½"
Sole (toe to heel):	1½"

No.7.
Socks with diagonal openwork broken rib. Picot-edged top and shaped foot (antique style)
(See photograph and measurements on previous page)

Materials:
1 (20 gram) ball Cotton Thread No. 100.
1 pair Knitting Pins. Size 20.

Tension: 20 sts. & 22 rows to 1" over st.st.

Instructions:
Cast on 42 sts.
Work top for a picot-edged hem thus:
Row 1: Knit.   **Row 2:** K1, purl to last st, k1.
Rows 3-10: Repeat Rows 1 & 2 four times.
Row 11: K1, * yf, sl1, k, psso, repeat from * to last st, k1.
Row 12: K1, purl to last st, k1.
Rows 13-22: Repeat Rows 1 & 2 five times.
Rows 23 & 24: Repeat Rows 11 & 12 once.
Change to pattern:
lst Row: Knit.
2nd, 4th & 6th Rows: K1, purl to last st, k1.
3rd & 5th Rows: Repeat Row 11.
Repeat these 6 rows of pattern - 6 times, decreasing 1 st at either side of 5th and 6th rows of last repeat. (38 sts.)

Divide for instep:
Change to stocking stitch to complete sock.
K28, turn,
K1, p16, k1. turn,
Work a further 14 rows on these centre 18 sts.
Shape for top of toe: Decrease 1 st at either side of next 4 knit rows. (10 sts). Work 3 rows straight.
Shape for sole under toe: Increase 1 st at either side of next 4 knit rows. (18 sts). Work 3 rows straight.
Shape for undersole and extension into ankle: Increase 1 st at either side of next and every 4th row until 30 sts are on needle.
Next row: K1, purl to last st, k1.   Cast off.

To complete heel : With right side of work facing you, join thread to 10 sts remaining on lefthand needle. Knit to end.

Next row: K.l, purl 9, (reverse the 10 sts carefully on other needle so that the needle point is at the outer edge) and work across these 10 sts, p9, k1. (20 sts on needle and centre back open seam is in the centre of your knitting).
Work 14 rows straight on these 20 sts.
Next row: K8, sl1, k1, psso, k2tog, k8.
Continue to decrease two sts in centre of next 2 knit rows. (14 sts). Cast off.

To make up:

To form antique style heel and foot section of this sock, work thus:
With right sides together,
Pin base of heel (underfoot) together by folding cast off edge in half. Stitch cast off edge together.
Pin either side of heel to cast off edge of underfoot (fitting up to top side of instep). (Stretch to fit if necessary). Stitch seam.
Pin each side of shaped instep edges to shaped sides of underfoot from ankle to toe. Stitch seam.

Return to leg section of sock, and with right sides together: Pin back seam edges, matching pattern rows and picot-edge top. Stitch back seam.

To form picot-edged top hem: Fold top to wrong side along first line of holes. Slipstitch cast-on edge loosely just above second line of holes. Turn sock to right side and press.

SOCK No. 8

**Socks with openwork mesh.
Ribbed top and simple heel.**

To fit a 11" Doll
or Doll with approx. leg and foot measurements:

Around Calf:	3"
Around Ankle:	2½"
Instep (centre leg to toe):	¾"
Ankle to Floor:	½"
Knee Joint to Floor (side):	2½"
Sole (toe to heel):	1⅜"

No.8
Socks with openwork mesh.
Ribbed top and simple heel.
(See photograph and measurements on page opposite)

Materials: Small quantity from
1 (5 gram) ball Cotton Thread No. 40.
1 pair Knitting Pins. Size 16.

Tension: 12 sts and 16 rows to 1" over st st.

Instructions:
Cast on 28 sts.
Work 8 rows in k1, p1 rib.
Next row: K1, * yf, k2tog, repeat from * to last st, k1.
Repeat this row 18 times.

Divide for foot:
K10, pattern 8, turn, Pattern 8, turn.
Continue to work a further 8 more pattern rows on centre 8 sts. Break thread.
With right side of work facing you, rejoin thread at base of instep, pick up and knit 5 sts along side of instep, k8 across centre, pick up and knit 5 sts down other side of instep, k10 from lefthand needle. (38 sts)
Next row: K1, purl to last st, k1.
Work a further 6 rows in st st.
Decrease for sole:
Next row: K1, sl1, k1, psso, k14, sl1, k1, psso, k2tog, k14, k2tog, k1.
Next row: K1, sl1 purlwise, p1, psso, p12, sl1 purlwise, p1, psso, p2tog, p12, p2tog, k1.
Next row: K1, sl1, k1, psso, k10, sl1, k1, psso, k2tog, k10, k2tog, k1.
Next row: K1, sl1 purlwise, p1, psso, p8, sl1 purlwise, p1, psso, p2tog., p8, p2tog, k1.
Cast off.

To make up:

With right sides together, pin back and undersole seam. Stitch seam. Turn to right side and press.

SOCK No.9

Socks with diagonal openwork rib. Ribbed top and simple heel.

To fit a 9"/10" Doll
or Doll with approx. leg and foot measurements:
Around Calf:	2½"
Around Ankle:	2¼"
Instep (centre leg to toe):	¾"
Ankle to Floor:	½"
Knee Joint to Floor (side):	2"
Sole (toe to heel):	1¼"

No.9
Socks with diagonal fancy rib.
Ribbed top and simple heel.
(See photograph and measurements on page opposite)

Materials:
1 (5 gram) ball Cotton Thread No. 80.
1 pair Knitting Pins. Size 20.

Tension: 18 sts & 22 rows to 1" over st st.

Instructions:
Cast on 34 sts.
Work 12 rows in k1, p1 rib.
Change to pattern:
Row 1: K2, * k1, sl1, k1, psso, yf, repeat from * to last 2 sts., k2.
Row 2: K1, purl to last st, k1.
Repeat these two rows of pattern 16 times.
Divide for foot:
Change to stocking stitch:
K24, turn,
K1, p12, k1, turn,
Work a further 10 rows on centre 14 sts.
Break thread.

With right side of work facing you, rejoin thread to base of instep where 10 sts were left on righthand needle - pick up and knit 6 sts along instep, k14 sts across centre, pick up and knit 6 sts along other side of instep, k10 sts. from lefthand needle. (46 sts.)
Next row: K1, purl to last st, k1.
Work 10 rows straight.
Next row: K1, k2tog, k18, k2tog (twice), k18, k2tog, k1.
Next row: K1, p2tog, p16, p2tog (twice), p16, p2tog, k1.
Next row: K1, k2tog, k14, k2tog (twice), k14, k2tog, k1.
Next row: K1, p2tog, p12, p2tog (twice), p12, p2tog, k1.
Next row: K1, k2tog, k10, k2tog (twice), k10, k2tog, k1.
Next row: K1, p2tog, p8, p2tog (twice) p8, p2tog, k1. (22 sts). Cast off.

To make up:
With right sides together, join back and undersole seam. Turn sock to right side and press.

SOCK No.10

**Socks with contrast stripes.
Ribbed top and simple heel.**

To fit a 7" Doll
or Doll with approx. leg and foot
measurements:

Around Calf:	2"
Around Ankle:	1³/₄"
Instep (centre leg to toe):	¹/₂"
Ankle to Floor:	³/₈"
Knee Joint to Floor (side):	1³/₄"
Sole (toe to heel):	1"

No.10
Socks with contrast stripes.
Ribbed top and simple heel.
(See photograph and measurements on page opposite)

Materials:
Small quantity of Cotton Thread No. 80 in white and small quantity of contrast for stripes.
1 pair Knitting Pins. Size 20.

Tension: 18 sts and 22 rows to 1" over st.st.

Instructions:
Cast on 30 sts.
Work 10 rows in k1, p1 rib.
Change to st st and work 16 rows in stripes, (2 rows white, 2 rows contrast).

Shape for foot:
K21 turn,
K1, p10, k1, turn,
Work 12 rows in stripes on centre 12 sts.
Break threads.
With right side of work facing you, rejoin white thread at base of instep, pick up and knit 6 sts up righthand side of instep, k12 sts across centre, pick up and knit 6 sts down lefthand side of instep, k9 sts from other needle. (42 sts)
Continue to finish foot in white only.
Work 5 rows straight in st st.

Shape undersole:
Decrease 1 st at either end and k2tog twice in the centre of each of the next 4 rows. Cast off.

To make up:

With right sides tog, stitch undersole and back seam taking care to match stripes up leg. Turn to right side and press.

(Note: For similar socks to fit a 10" doll, follow this Pattern but use No.16 knitting pins and No.40 cotton thread. The tension will be 12 sts and 16 rows to 1" over st st.

ABBREVIATIONS

st (sts)	stitch (stitches)
K k	Knit
P p	Purl
tog	together
foll	following
dec	decrease
inc	increase
alt	alternate
"	measurement in inches
cm	centimetres (metric)
mm	millimetres (metric)
psso	pass slipped stitch over
sl	slip (move st from left to right needle without working)
approx	approximately
st st	stocking stitch (knit one row, purl one row)
garter st	knit every row
yf	yarn forward (see page 9)

For North American readers:

Cast off	Bind off
Tension	Gauge
Stocking Stitch	Stockinette Stitch.

Needle Sizes:

Size 16	3.0s
Size 18	4.0s
Size 20	5.0s

CONVERSION INTO METRIC.

All the measurements in this book are in inches. For your convenience the following table converts inches into centimetres.

Leg and foot measurements:

6¾"	17 cm	5½"	14 cm
6½"	16.5 cm	5"	12.75 cm
6"	15.25 cm		
4¾"	12 cm	3¾"	9.5 cm
4½"	11.5 cm	3½"	9 cm
4¼"	10.75 cm	3¼"	8.25 cm
4"	10 cm	3"	7.5 cm
2¾"	7 cm	1¾"	4.5 cm
2½"	6.25 cm	1½"	3.75 cm
2⅜"	6 cm	1⅜"	3.5 cm
2¼"	5.75 cm	1¼"	3 cm
2"	5 cm	1"	2.5 cm
¾"	2.75 cm	⅝"	1.5 cm
½"	1.25 cm		

Doll measurements (head to toe):

26"	66 cm	22/24"	56/61 cm
20/21"	51/53 cm	18/19"	46/48 cm
16"	41 cm	15"	38 cm
13/14"	33/35 cm	11"	28 cm
9/10"	23/25 cm	7"	18 cm

MATERIALS

Fine knitting needles:
Sizes 14, 16, 18, 20 (and also 22) in pairs with knobs at one end, or sets of 4 with double points.

Crochet cotton thread:
Thicknesses of 20, 40, 60, 80 and 100 in white and shades of ecru and cream.
Thicknesses of 20, 40 and 80 are also available in a variety of colours.

If you have difficulty in obtaining any of the knitting pins or thread mentioned in this book and shown in the photographs on the front and back covers, they can be obtained from:

Joan Nerini
20 Court Close
Patcham,
Brighton, East Sussex, BN1 8YG
England.

Please send three first class stamps for full details.
(For overseas enquiries, please send international postal vouchers)

NOTES

Please use this space to keep a record of any alterations you may wish to make.